Warriors

An Aleyo's guide to the care and maintenance of "Warriors"

William J. Irizarry Jr.
Awo Ni Orunmila, Iwori Rote, Ifa Ala

Copyright © 2012 by William J. Irizarry Jr.
Edited by Efun Yomi & Òggún Lari

All Rights Reserved. No portion of this publication may be reproduced or transmitted in any form by any means, electronic or mechanical, including photocopying, recording, or any information storage or retrieval system, without permission in writing from the author of this book.

Second Edition 2012

Printed in the United States of America

ISBN-10: 1468155539
ISBN-13: 978-1468155532

Table of Contents

Introduction	5
About the Author	6-7
What is an Aleyo	8
What is an Aborisha	8
Who are the Warriors	8
Eshu	9
Òggún	10
Ochosi	11
Osun	12
What the "Warriors" do for us	13
Why do we receive "Warriors"	14
Can anyone receive "Warriors"	14
How to care and service the "Warriors"	15
Cleaning	15
Light	16
Libation	16
Addimu	17
Where in the home should your "Warriors" be	18
Adding Toys and other items to Eshu	19
Adding Implements to Òggún	20
Picking your "Warriors" up	20
Moving	20

Ebo	21
Ebo Eje	21
Entrada	22
Communicating with your "Warriors"	22
Speaking directly to them	22
Obi Divination	23
Can anyone touch them	23
Does having "Warriors" brings spirits	24
Menstruation	24
Sex and nudity	25
Being sick	25
Working your "Warriors"	26
Supplies	26
What you should know about your Ceremony	27
What you should know about your godfather	28
Words of advice	28-31
The role and responsibility of a godparent	32
the role and responsibility of a godchild	32
Vocabulary	33-34
Photos	35-39
Notes	40

Introduction

Ggogbo Iboru Iboya Ibosise

This book was originally intended for my Ahijados (Godchildren) however as time progressed my vision shifted a bit. I wish to educate and enlightening the average Aleyo/Aborisha and hopefully refreshing the minds of others. Tending to ones "Warriors" is a simple task that at times we neglect. Receiving Orisa is nothing less than an honor and should be respected as such. With receiving Orisa comes responsibility and obligation, a matter not to be taken lightly. It is our duty to care for them as they care for us.

The information that follows pertains to the Lucumi tradition also known as Santeria. With that said please enjoy the following and remember each Ile (house) is different, what you read here should be taken into consideration but should not be taken as law. Consult with those whom represent you in the religion i.e. Godparents.

William J. Irizarry Jr.
Awó Ni Òrúnmìlà - Iwori Rote - Ifá Alá

About the Author

Born and raised in New York City of Puerto Rican decent William J. Irizarry Jr. was introduced to the mysteries of Orisa by his first Padrino (Godfather) Cuban born and former Chef to Fidel Castro, Babalorisa Ramon Torres Olo Obatala Ibae. William grew up in the New York City Housing Projects where his spent the majority of his upbringing with childhood Friend/Cousin Alexander LaSalle founder and musical director of Alma Moya, precisionists, singer, song writer and Bakonfula in the Palo Mayombe tradition. Alexander introduced William to the drum and music in general which they played for hours on end at all times of the day and night practicing Orisa and Eggun songs. It was Williams love for music that illuminated his path and fueled his desire in becoming an Aborisha. William was officially initiated into the Lucumi tradition at the age of fourteen when he received his Elekes/Collares (Beads), Orisa Olokun and Ibeji from Iyaloricha Maria Latimar Olo Yemaya of the Bronx. Less than one year later at the age of fifteen William received Awofaka (Mano de Orula) and Warriors (Orisa's Eshu, Òggún, Ochosi and Osun) from Cuban Born Oluwo Moises Montesion OyekuPica of

New York City. Three years later at the age of eighteen William traveled to Santos Suarez, Cuba where he was initiated in the mysteries of both Ocha and Ifa. August 1998 William J. Irizarry Jr. became Oluwo Awo Ni Orunmila, Iwori Rote, Ifa Ala godson of Oluwo Alberto Ofun Nalbe and Ojubon Oretes Ogbe Bara a first generation Babalawo within his family. Three months later William received Kuanaldo and Osain. William has dedicated his life to the study of Ifa and Orisa teachings picking up and mastering the art of traditional beading along the way. William credits his love of art and beadwork from attending a beading seminar by artist Manny Vega hosted by the Caribbean Cultural Center in New York City and his love of music from his childhood friend Alexander LaSalle. Presently William is under the expert tutelage of Olofista Emilio Ogbe Unle of Orlando Florida where he continues his lifelong study of Ifa and Orisa teaching passing his knowledge onto his godchildren as well as his love of art and music.

What is an Aleyo?

By definition an Aleyo is an outsider, a new comer. An Aleyo is someone who has not been initiated as a priest. A person may have received Elekes (Collares/Beads), Warriors, Olokun and Ibeji and or other Orisa however is still considered an Aleyo because he/she is not crowned.

What is an Aborisha?

First and foremost please play close attention to the follow definition, many become confused with its meaning. An Aborisha very simply is someone who follows the way of the Orisa. To say that your religion or belief is Orisa based is a personal choice; such a decision makes a person an Aborisha. However an Aborisha is still considered an Aleyo because he or she has not been initiated as a priest.

Who are the "Warriors"?

The warriors are a set of 4 principal Orisa; Eshu (Eleggua), Òggún, Ochosi and Osun. The following are brief descriptions of each Principal Orisa:

Eshu (Eleggua)

Eshu is the divine messenger of Olodumare (God); he represents the element of opportunity and the possibility of change. Eshu is often perceived as an adolescent as he is very playful and a trickster by nature however make no mistake Ehsu an adult Orisa. Eshu represents the crossroads and is the opener and closer of all doors and paths both literal and figuratively. Eshu is honored first in all ceremonies therefore Monday is Eshu's day, 3/21 are his numbers, June 13th is his feast day and red and black are his colors. Eshu has many manifestations often in the form of cement mass with cowry shell for eyes mouth and ears. Other forms include but are not limited to carved wooden Figures, large sea shells and simple stones. There is no Eshu without a stone; the stone represents Eshu's natural form and contains his spirit within.

Favorite Foods

Dried Ekute/Jutia
Dried Fish
Toasted Corn
Cigars and Tobacco
Rum

Honey
Popcorn
Coconut
All fruit
Cake
Guava
Boiled or baked Yam
Cornmeal Balls both raw and cooked
Epo

Òggún

Òggún is the Orisa of war, industry, technology, he is the blacksmith, the patron of all those who work with metals, doctors, surgeons, carpenters etc. Òggún brought the art of iron smelting to the world. Òggún taught mankind how to fend for themselves. Òggún taught mankind how to hunt, how to carve, and how to build. Òggún is the great warrior, the representation of brute strength. Òggún clears the path so it may be explored. Òggún is a forest Orisa his number is 7, colors are black and green, feast day is June 29th and day of the week is Tuesday (the day of victory). Òggún is represented in the "Warrior" set as the cauldron, the stone, and seven tools contained within.

Favorite Foods

Both roasted and baked Yams
Baked Fish
Salt & Pepper
Palm Wine
Rum
Chamba
Toasted Corn & Toasted Beans
Epo
Watermelon
Coconut
Name
Ginger
Mangos

Ochosi

Ochosi is the great hunter, the great archer. Ochosi represents justice and is often the patron of the accused. Ochosi like Òggún is a forest Orisa, a great seer, a great magician healer and warrior. Without Ochosi the world would not eat. Ochosi also shares Tuesday's with Òggún, his colors are blue and amber, feast day is October 25th and number is also 7. Ochosi is represented in the "Warrior" set by the bow and arrow.

Favorite Foods

Coconuts
Baked and raw fish
Anisette
Almonds
plate of 7 different beans
Cactus
Dear steaks
All Fruit
Epo
Rum

Osun

Osun in the "Warrior" set is represented by a metal staff adorned with a rooster or bird. Osun is a guardian Orisa who is forever vigilant protecting and warning the recipient. Osun is an Ifa Orisa who is very mystical and sacred to Babalawos. The four bells represent the four winds, the four columns that sustain our world and home. To an Aleyo/Aborisha Osun represents the recipient more specifically the Ori (Head) or spiritual head of the recipient. Should Osun fall either on its own or by the hands of the recipient one should take heed as this is an early warning sign of danger looming. A consultation should follow any instance where Osun falls in an effort to remedy the situation, if any. Osun shares June 29th as a feast day with Òggún.

Favorite Foods

Coco butter
Rice
Ekute/Jutia
Toasted Corn
Dried Fish
Cascaria
Epo
Honey

What the "Warriors" do for us

Receiving the warriors is one of the most important steps in the Lucumi tradition. Your warriors are exactly that "Warriors" they are your defenders. They will assist you in coming closer to understanding you path is this life. They will give you the guidance and strength needed to walk your path, forever vigilant, forever at guard for you.

Why do we receive "Warriors"?

Normally it is marked in a reading with either an Olorisa or Babalawo that one must receive warriors or there can be a situation where it would benefit a person to receive them. Receiving "Warriors" is traditionally the second step one takes in the religion after receiving Elekes (Collares/Beads) however depending on the circumstances this is not always the case.

Can anyone receive "Warriors"?

Absolutely! If it has been recommended or marked via divination or benefits a person, anyone of any faith, religion or ethnicity can receive Orisa. As mentioned in the introduction of this book receiving Orisa is nothing less than an honor. With receiving Orisa comes responsibility and obligation, a matter not to be taken lightly.

How to care and service the "Warriors"

Every Monday the following is preformed:

1. **Cleaning** – As with cleaning any Orisa cold water is a must, never hot. This can be done either at the sink or utilizing a pale or bucket of water. An alternative to cleaning Eshu with water would be to use white rum and cotton (old fashioned way). Once Eshu is clean and dry rub him with Epo (Manteca Corojo/Palm Oil). Òggún/Ochosi are generally left "as is" they are warriors and like to remain a bit grimy. Most practitioners simply remove all feathers (if being fed animals) and leave the blood to dry. Occasionally you may wipe Òggún/Ochosi down with Epo to prevent their tools from rusting simultaneously giving them a nice sheen. Osun should always be kept clean; cold water will do the trick.

    Note: Never use soap or detergents on any Orisa

2. **Light**- A single candle is lit for the "Warriors" either a small white sabot candle or 7day glass candle. When offering a candle present it to your Ori (head), bless yourself with it and place it in front of your "Warriors". When lighting the candle say either out loud or to yourself "As I illuminate this candle may you illuminate my path so that I may see all that is in front of me and nothing may be hidden, As I give you light, give me light, as I give you strength give me strength.

3. **Libation** – Every Monday when servicing your "Warriors" a Jicara with cold water is offered. This cold water is a refreshing element essential to all offerings. At this point you will begin to Moyuba/Mojuba. Mojuba by definition is a pray/invocation/Paying homage. You are to take the Jicara filled with cold water in your left hand with your right hand (Middle and Ring finger) sprinkle a few drops on each Orisa beginning with Eshu. Simple Mojuba is as follows: *" Omi Tutu, Ona Tutu, Tutu*

Laroye, Tutu Ile" Meaning: Refreshing water, Refresh my path, Refresh Eshu, Refresh the home". A sample of a longer pray: *"Mojuba Olofin, Mojuba Olodumare, Mojuba gbogbo irunmole, Mojuba gbogbo Orisa, Omi Tutu, Ona Tutu, Tutu Laroye, Tutu Ile*…etc. The simple Mojuba above is a universal basic pray used by all Aborisha.

4. **Addimu** (Food Offerings) – To Eshu offerings of candy, Rum, Tobacco and Epo are standard the same is so for Òggún/Ochosi minus candy (Remember each Ile is different). When offering rum, it is given from the mouth. To do this take some rum into your mouth but do not swallow, spray (not spit) rum onto Eshu then Òggún/Ochosi. Osun should not be given Rum; Osun is to be ever vigilant, Rum would defeat his purpose. A cigar can be offered either lit or unlit. Offering tobacco is also given from the mouth, experienced practitioners will place a lit cigar into their mouth backwards and blow smoke onto Eshu, Òggún/Ochosi and Osun (be very careful doing this). To Osun with

the exception of Rum offerings of Tobacco, Rice, Cascaria, Ori (coco butter) and Eku, Eya, Agbado are standard.

Note: If your Eshu, Òggún/Ochosi appear orange after you have rubbed them with Epo, you're using too much. You should only use just enough to coat them lightly leaving a decent shine.

Additional Offerings include Honey, coffee, Coconuts, Popcorn pastries and special cooked dishes. Refer to you godparents for prepared food recipes.

Where in the home should the "Warriors" be?

Traditionally Eshu Òggún/Ochosi and Osun are kept by the door either just behind the door, off to the side or facing the door however at times living conditions may not permit this. Osun is kept up high and away where he is less likely to fall. Also Osun should be facing the main entrance to the home. If the recipient has received Awofaka or Ikofafun (Mano de Orula)

Osun is kept next to it. Some may dedicate a special room for the Orisa (Orisa room) or an alter type setup in a room or bedroom. A bedroom is not a great idea as at some point you will be naked or become involved in sexual activities, this will be discussed later on. Some practitioners will purchase a cabinet either open faced or with doors, this is acceptable.

Adding toys and other items to Eshu

Adding toys and other items to your Eshu is normal; Eshu loves toys and other items. However keep in mind spoiling your Eshu rotten is not a great idea. Food for thought; imagine having a two year old and spoiling that child rotten giving him/her everything and anything he/she desired. Now imagine out of the blue cutting back or not giving that child anything. The same way a two year old would catch a fit is the same way Eshu will react. So, adding toys and other items should be done in moderation.

Adding Implements to Òggún

Keep in mind that Òggún is the Orisa of Iron and industry, everything and anything comprised of metal belongs to him. That said, aside from the tools received with Òggún addition tools may be added. At times and for certain reasons Òggún may request an item or items to be added. Each tool or item represents something or has specific meaning. Often in a reading Òggún may ask for something or ask to be re-enforced. Adding items on your own is "ok" however Òggún must be asked whether he wants the item or not. In addition each item that is added to Òggún must be washed in Omiero.

Picking your "Warriors" up

Whenever you pick an Orisa up at anytime weather to move them a few inches or across the room, you must say "Ago". Saying "Ago" is asking permission, out of respect.

Moving

Moving or relocating to a new home with your "Warriors" can be task at times but it doesn't have to be. Very simply you want to make sure the "Warriors" a placed in a sturdy box or container for the ride, Osun should remain upright at all times. From experience flying with your "Warriors" is not that uncommon as one might think however there are a few things you should know. Prior to 9/11 passengers were able to bring their "Warriors" as carry on. Post 9/11 this is not possible, unfortunately due to airports high Security standards Eshu, Òggún/Ochosi and Osun will have to fly in a suitcase under the plan. The Orisa understand this and it is "ok".

Ebo

As an Aleyo/Aborisha you will hear this word used often. Ebo by definition is "sacrifice" whether its food, time, money, material or animal. Typical Ebo's consist of Addimu (food) or material items.

Ebo Eje (Blood Sacrifice)

Ebo Eje by definition is a "blood" sacrifice of an animal of some sort to be determined via divination. Ebo Eje is always a last resort after all other possibilities have been explored. Ebo Eje is to be performed only by a competent

Olorisa or Babalawo whom has been properly trained in such matters.

Entrada (Entrance)

Entrada is a ceremony in which the "Warriors" are fed in the home after they are initially received. Entrada is traditionally done within three months after you've receive your "Warriors". Entrada is also traditionally preformed after moving to a new location. Entrada is very simple and is essentially strengthening your "Warriors" and letting them know that where they eat is where they live.

Communicating with your "warriors"

- Speaking directly to your "warriors"

It is essential that you form a relationship with your warriors, confide in them, speak to them either out loud or to yourself. Tell them about your day, your life what problems you're facing, what your goals and aspiration are. Do this always during your Monday service or at anytime but remember Orisa are not magical genie lamps that your rub and make wishes. One should NEVER approach an Orisa upset or angry, this is taboo.

- Obi divination

Obi divination very simply put is method of communicating with the Orisa utilizing four pieces of coconut that are cast onto the ground were signs/patterns appear and are interpreted by the diviner. Ultimately these signs/patterns are interpreted with the goal of ascertaining either a yes or no answer. Due to its complexity, Obi divination should not be attempted by the inexperienced. Some Ile's prohibit Aleyos/Aborisha from casting Obi on the other hand some Iles will teach those willing to learn. If you feel the need or have questions for your warriors speak with your Godparents they will find the best course of action.

Can Anyone Touch Them?

Generally speaking no one other than the recipient and godparent(s) should touch or handle the "Warriors". The only exception to this rule would be if you, the recipient, gave permission to do so. Circumstances in which this may occur are; extremely ill or unable to physically move them.

Does having the "Warriors" in the home bring spirits?

Recipients of the "Warriors" and even family members may experience events such as missing items, rearranged objects, food falling on the ground etc. These are all manifestations of Eshu and should not be mistaken for malicious activity, this is his nature. Many practitioners will also experience eye winks, smiles and smirks from their Eshu, again this is all normal. The "Warriors", Eshu in particular, will let you they're there one way or another. As far as spirits are concerned, Orisa are on a different plain all together. If you are seeing shadows and experiencing anything other than the above mentioned it's time to consult with your godparents and figure out exactly what's going on.

Menstrual Cycle

With respect to women, during your menstrual cycle it is taboo for you to handle your "Warriors". Once your cycle has ended you may resume your service. This is also the case after you have given birth; you must wait until after hemorrhaging has ceased to continue your service. The Orisa understand this so missing a Monday service is "ok".

Sex and Nudity

Sex in front or around Orisa is taboo, a serious "NO NO" hence the reason for not having your Orisa in the bedroom. Had you just engaged in a sexual act, wash up before handling Orisa or wait until the next day, it is always best to be pure before handling Orisa. With respects to nudity, the Orisa understand that we were born naked and being naked is natural however this is another taboo.

Being sick

Traditionally speaking one should not service the "Warriors" when sick. Its best to wait until one is physically healthy enough to properly care for them, they understand so don't worry about them being upset with you. If you find yourself spiritually sick then it's time to consult with those who represent you.

Working your "Warriors"

Working your Warrior's refers to trabajos, Ebos and brujeria utilizing your warriors in an effort resolve any given situation. Remember you're "Warriors" or any Orisa for that matter are not magical Genie Lamps that your rub and make wishes on. That said your "Warriors" can be worked in an infinite number of ways however what's good for the goose is not always good for that gander. What is good for someone else may not be good for you. Have a conversation with your godparent(s); let them know what's going on if need be have a reading so a proper Ebo can be marked. You want to work your "Warriors" in the best and most efficient way possible to untimely produce the best result.

Supplies

The following is a set of basic supplies an Aleyo/Aborisha should have on hand:

- Jicara (at least one)
- Epo
- Oti

- Oni
- Eku, Eya, Agbado (can be purchased mixed together)
- Candles (plane white)
- Candy
- Efun
- Ori

The aforementioned items can be purchased at your local Botanica.

What you should know about your Ceremony

-Date

-Location

-Path of Eshu received

-Godfathers information

-Instruction on care and maintenance

What you should know about your Godfather

You should know your Godfathers:

-First and last name

-Odu Ifa (if a Babalawo)

-Guardian Angel and accompanying Orisa

-Years of initiation

-Ifa birthday (If a Babalawo) Ocha birthday (if an Olorisa)

-Contact information

Words of Advice

1. Always remember Orisa are divinities and not magical Genie's.

2. Eshu likes to travel, if possible take him to the park, the porch, a walk, your job etc.

3. Òggún's tools should not be lying down or just thrown inside his pot instead they should be standing up with the business end pointing upward. The same is so for

Ochosi's bow and arrow. Òggún is an Orisa who works 24/7 having his tools lying down would defeat his purpose.

4. When you first receive your Eshu he will appear very clean and the cement very light. As time passes and with service your Eshu will change in color becoming darker and smooth. Don't panic this is normal.

5. Should you yourself fall and or bump your head speak with your godparents. When we fall and or bump or heads it is sometimes necessary to have our head rogated (referring to Rogacion de cabeza) and in some cases fead alongside Osun.

6. Cleaning your Eshu with water or rum does not have to be done every Monday. The day after an Ebo Eje yes, however during normal service it is not necessary. Typically there are four Mondays a month, pick one and clean him with water or rum.

7. Eshu likes money! Offer money to Eshu whether in dollar bills or coins. If you having financial difficulties Eshu can

defiantly help you in that area. Whatever money you offer to your Eshu do not remove unless you plan to use that money to buy him something. You never want to find yourself in dept with Eshu.

8. Chips, cracks and falls. If your Eshu for some odd reason falls and sustains a crack or chip don't panic. Contact your godfather and let him know exactly what happened. Nine times of out ten the damage can be repaired and Eshu appeased.

9. Aleyo and Aborisha should be aware there are two types of "Warriors", "Warriors" given by an Olorisa and "Warriors" given by a Babalawo. This is a very sensitive topic as there has been much debate regarding which type to receive. Due to this topics sensitive nature I will be brief.

Although both are beneficial should one decide to receive "Warriors" from a Babalawo you should know only a Babalawo can feed and touch those "Warriors". Olorisa cannot feed

"Warriors" given by a Babalawo. Babalawo on the other hand can feed both types. Ile's that function without Babalawos tend to only give "Warriors" from an Olorisa, in other words "Warriors " they can work with. That said; consult with your godparents for further input on the topic. My advice to you is to weigh your options, understand the difference and why. It may be a good idea to have a conversation with both a Babalawo and Olorisa and see what they have to say. As I tell my Ahijados "Exercise your right to be informed"

10. Never abandon your Orisa! Should you find yourself unable or unwilling to care for them, call your godfather and hew will pick them up or make other arrangements.

11. Never Kneel in front of your Eshu you will understand why the day you receive you're "Warriors". It would be inappropriate for me to divulge such information. Sitting in front of your "Warriors" is the norm.

The role and responsibility of a Godparent

Your godparent should be available to you should you him/her. He or she should be someone you can turn to for spiritual guidance as well as life lessons period. Your godparent should be able to teach you about what you will or have received how to properly care for it and the protocols and procedures that follows.

The role and responsibility of a Godchild

The role of a godchild remains the same across the board, whether a godchild of an Olorisha or Babalawo. As a godchild you should remain open-minded and receptive to suggestion and direction. Always respect your godparent's status regardless of age, gender or orientation as well as the rules and regulations of the Ile. Once you become a godchild it is required that you address you godparent in the appropriate manner e.g. Oluwo Padrino Madrina etc. s

Vocabulary

1. Epo – Manteca Corojo – Palm Oil
2. Oti – Aquadiente/Rum
3. Oni – Honey
4. Eku – Dried Jutia
5. Eya – Dried Fish
6. Agbado/Awado – Toasted Corn
7. Ori – Dual meaning 1. Head 2. Coco butter
8. Efun – Cascaria
9. Ebo – Sacrifice
10. Ebo Eje – Blood Sacrifice
11. Addimu – Food Offering
12. Obi – Coconut
13. Atana – Candle
14. Jicara – Half Calabash
15. Ile – house
16. Omi – Water
17. Mojuba/Moyuba- Prayer/Invocation/paying homage
18. Omi Tutu – Fresh Water
19. Asha – Cigar
20. Omiero – Herbal mixture that has been consecrated by either an Olorisa or Babalawo.

21. Babalawo – Babalawo (Father of Secrets) High Priest within the Lucumi and Traditional Yoruba traditions.
22. Olorisa – Priest within the Lucumi tradition.
23. Lucumi – Literally meaning "friend" is the term practitioners, of what was formerly know as Santeria, use to identify their faith/religion.
24. Orisa – A deity, God or Goddess, a manifestation of Olodumare (God) within the Lucumi and traditional Yoruba traditions.
25. Rogated – Refers to "Rogacion de Cabeza" or Ebo Leri. Cleansing of the head through sacrifice.
26. Osode – Reading
27. Chamba – Extremely potent, extremely hot and spicy rum infused with hot peppers, rum and many other fundamental ingredients. Offered to Eggun and select Orisa. Also utilized in the Palo and Vodu traditions.

Orlando, FL 2009

Òggún De Babalawo, Orlando FL 2007

Bronx, NY 2009

Orlando, FL 2009

Orlando, FL 2009

Orlando, FL 2009

Bronx, NY 2009

Notes

Ito Iban Eshu

Made in the USA
Monee, IL
05 July 2020